Acknowledgements

Thanks to the many children and young people we have known over the years who have intrigued, inspired and impressed us. Thanks for the pioneering work of Elizabeth Newson without whom we would not be where we are in our journey towards understanding the complexities of Pathological Demand Avoidance syndrome (PDA). We would also like to acknowledge the insights given to us by numerous parents of children and young people with PDA.

Thanks to friends, family, colleagues and JKP for their support in turning this idea into a book. Thanks too to Judy Gould for writing a foreword and to Jonathon Powell for his illustrations.

Can I tell you about Pathological Demand Avoidance syndrome?

Can I tell you about...?

The "Can I tell you about...?" series offers simple introductions to a range of limiting conditions and other issues that affect our lives. Friendly characters invite readers to learn about their experiences, the challenges they face, and how they would like to be helped and supported. These books serve as excellent starting points for family and classroom discussions.

Other subjects covered in the "Can I tell you about...?" series

Can I tell you about Pathological Demand Avoidance syndrome?

A guide for friends, family and professionals

RUTH FIDLER AND PHIL CHRISTIE
Foreword by Judith Gould
Illustrated by Jonathon Powell

Jessica Kingsley *Publishers*
London and Philadelphia

First published in 2015
by Jessica Kingsley Publishers
73 Collier Street
London N1 9BE, UK
and
400 Market Street, Suite 400
Philadelphia, PA 19106, USA

www.jkp.com

Copyright © Ruth Fidler and Phil Christie 2015
Illustrations copyright © Jonathon Powell 2015
Foreword copyright © Judith Gould 2015

Library of Congress Cataloging in Publication Data
A CIP catalog record for this book is available from the Library of Congress

British Library Cataloguing in Publication Data
A CIP catalogue record for this book is available from the British Library

ISBN 978 1 84905 513 0
eISBN 978 0 85700 929 6

Printed and bound in Great Britain
by Bell and Bain Ltd, Glasgow

Contents

Foreword

In recent years there has been a greater awareness of individuals who have been described as having a pattern of behaviour named Pathological Demand Avoidance syndrome (PDA). It is now recognised that this condition is part of the autism spectrum. The behaviours diagnostic of an autism spectrum disorder are shown in many manifestations and overlap with the behaviours of PDA. Individuals with this pattern of behaviour, like others on the autism spectrum, share difficulties with social interaction, social communication and social imagination (known as the triad of impairments) together with a rigid, repetitive lifestyle. The key is the social aspects of interaction, communication and imagination. In people with PDA, extreme demand avoidance stands out as one of the main defining features.

Children with PDA are often more intellectually able and verbally articulate than children with more typical autism and also appear to be more socially aware. However, they have major problems in relating to and understanding the subtle social aspects of life, together with the unwritten rules of social interaction. They can be extremely challenging but understanding the nature of their difficulties can really make a difference to their lives. This book offers just such an understanding.

The first part of the book is written from the perspective of Issy, who is 11 years old and has PDA. She explains how she sees the world relating to her strengths and difficulties. Issy's perceptions and descriptions give us insight into how she struggles to make others understand the way she copes and struggles with all aspects of her life and what she calls her PDA. She gives us her ideas about how the person with PDA can be helped.

The second part of the book gives management guidelines based on the authors' vast knowledge and experience in working with children with PDA.

As PDA is one condition on the autism spectrum, the authors point out that there is not one list of strategies exclusively for children with autism and another separate list for children with PDA. They overlap and many children need a combination of the two with individualised adaptations. However, it is useful to recognise the PDA pattern of behaviour as the "demand avoidance" dimension, together with the person's need to be in control; this does require a very specialised approach. Head-on confrontation has to be avoided wherever possible. Negotiation and compromise is most helpful. Whoever is working with the child needs to remain cool, detached, judicious and absolutely fair. The children cannot cope with strong emotions, whether in themselves or other people. Faced with emotion shown overtly they tend to become distressed, angry and negative in reaction.

The authors cover this aspect of the behavioural profile in detail.

For anyone working with individuals who maybe are not conforming to conventional social rules and who can be oppositional or just different, then this book is a must, as it gives a very sensible, pragmatic approach to helping and supporting such people.

Dr Judith Gould
Consultant clinical psychologist and director – The NAS
(National Autistic Society) Lorna Wing Centre for Autism

Introduction

The authors hope that this book will help children and adults understand more about Pathological Demand Avoidance syndrome (PDA). It is written in two parts. The first part is written from the perspective of a child, an 11-year-old girl called Issy, who explains what it is like for her to have PDA. The second part is written from the perspective of the authors who give information and strategies that in their experience can help support children with PDA.

You are probably reading this book because you either live or work with someone who is affected by PDA. They may be very like Issy, or her friend Alfie, or they may seem a bit different. Everyone with PDA will share the same aspects of their condition that impact on them. The way their life is affected will depend on their unique personality as well as lots of other things in their lives. No two people with PDA are quite the same. That's what makes them such great company!

We need to understand what PDA is to help us understand each individual with PDA. If we can do this, we will be able to support them better. Also, if children and young people with PDA can develop a better understanding of themselves, they will be able to manage various situations, make good relationships, learn, make wise decisions and build a positive future.

"Hello, my name is Issy. It's short for Isabella.
I am 11 and I live at home with my mum, dad, my
younger sister Alice, and my lovely cat Splodge."

"There are lots of things I can tell you about myself. I am a girl. I have brown hair. I am good at singing, although I only like to sing when I'm on my own. I wear glasses for watching TV and I like nail varnish.

We did a great 'all about me' project at school last week. I knew just what to say when they asked me what I'm good at. I told Mrs Jones, my teacher, that I'm really good at art and at singing. When she asked me who is important to me, I told her my family, my friends and of course Splodge. My family is really important to me, although I find it hard to tell them that, which is why I often draw them pictures to show them how much I love them. When Mrs Jones asked me about what I find difficult, I told her that I know that I have trouble doing what people ask me to do. I think she already knew that! I also said that often I don't know what other people are thinking or feeling, and that I can get confused about what to do or say when I'm playing with other children. When she asked me what sort of things bothered me I told her I hate loud noises, new shoes and sitting on the smelly floor in the school hall."

"I'm good at playing on my own. My favourite game is when I pretend to be a pop star."

"I watch YouTube to help me learn the dance moves to my favourite songs, and then I pretend I'm in my own music video. Sometimes when I'm pretending, I can forget that it's not real.

I like making greetings cards and I'm going to earn lots of money selling them one day. I have sold some to my family and at the school fair. Mum and Alice like to join in making them, which I don't mind as long as they stick to my ideas. After all it is my business. It's called Issy's Bizzy. Mum and Alice have signed a contract to prove that I'm the boss, to say what jobs they do and to say how much they will get paid. When I sell cards at the school fair, Mum and Alice work on the stall. They are very pleased to be able to help me and to earn some money at the same time. Last time, I told them that I couldn't work on the stall because I am the company boss. Actually there is another reason that I didn't tell them. It was because I was too shy, too worried about working out the money and too stressed about talking to people I don't know. I was feeling a bit sensitive that day."

"Sometimes Alfie builds Lego while I make cards, or we watch a film together. He has a giant trampoline in his garden and we have lots of fun jumping on it together."

"I like having friends. I have a friend at school. Her name is Emily and she has sat next to me in class all year. She lets me borrow her best felt-tips and I let her use my crayons. We talk about TV and pop music. I'm also friends with three other girls in my class but Emily is my special friend.

I have another friend out of school. His name is Alfie and he lives near my house. He is ten and his mum is my mum's friend. My mum told me that Alfie has PDA too. Although he's like me in some ways, he's different in others. I guess, even though we both have PDA, we are still individuals. Alfie and I don't disagree often, but when we do, we get really stuck and really grumpy with each other. I guess we are the same in that way. When that happens we find it very hard to co-operate with each other and one of us usually has to go home.

For me, co-operating with other people is a bit like struggling to walk down a stony path, even if there is something I want at the end of that path. Some days it feels as though I am walking down that path wearing comfy slippers and I can walk over the stones easily, even skip."

"Some days it's like I have sore feet and no shoes on. Moving forward on those days is really hard."

"I hate this feeling partly because it's really annoying if people expect me to cope on a bad day. I also hate the fact that deep down I wish I wasn't being difficult. I don't want to be difficult and I would like people to understand that about me.

Alfie used to go to an ordinary school but that didn't work out for him. I remember one day Alfie's mum came over to see my mum. I listened to them talking and I heard Alfie's mum crying because he had got really upset at school and had been throwing chairs and swearing at teachers and had run away. She was very worried about him and said that he would probably have to leave that school. Now he goes to a special school that he has to get to by taxi every day because it is so far away from home. He doesn't do his work in lessons like at an ordinary school; he does it in projects that he's interested in like Disney Pixar films and Lego. He has time on the trampoline or the cycling machine at school every day. He likes his new school but the other pupils live too far away to see them outside school so he likes spending time with me."

"Sometimes it doesn't last long when Alice
and I play together because Alice says
she feels I boss her about too much."

"You already know that I like art and singing. I also like to make up games. One of my favourite games is 'School of Dance' when I play that I am the teacher and that my toys are the pupils. I have a register for the pupils, I choose the music, I design the costumes and I make up the dances ready for filming music videos. I like to do it on my own but every now and then Alice joins in.

Alfie doesn't play pretend games. He prefers going out on his bike or building Lego.

He had a problem the other day when he went out on his bike to the park. He saw some kids who went to his old school so he went over to say hi. They told him to move because his bike was in the middle of their football game so he got upset that they didn't seem pleased to see him and he got into a fight. Alfie's dad had to take him round to the other boy's house later to talk to his family. When I play with Alfie, I prefer to stay at his house or at mine."

"There are some things about me that are really easy to see, like that I am a girl with brown hair who wears glasses. There are other things about me that you can't see just by looking at me. You need to get to know me before you understand me, or before you know that I have PDA.

Not many people have heard of PDA. PDA is a type of autism. Autism describes the way some people's brains work. It can't be seen just by looking at someone, but it does affect the way someone with autism thinks, talks and behaves. Autism affects different people in different ways so it is called the autism spectrum, which means that there is a range of ways people can experience it. It's called a spectrum because that means it's like a rainbow – full of different colours and shades.

People with autism spectrum conditions are likely to do some things differently from other people. They may:

- sometimes get confused about what other people do or say or are thinking

- not know how they feel in their body (like whether they are hungry or ill) or not know how they feel in their emotions (like whether they are happy, sad or angry)

- get confused about what to do or what to say when they talk to other people

- not like changes that they are not prepared for

- get stuck in doing things the same way

- be more sensitive to what they see, touch, taste, hear or smell.

People with PDA will also be affected by some of these things that are part of autism. It is all a bit complicated, isn't it? Don't worry, even some adults find it really hard to understand too.

Let me tell you some more. PDA stands for Pathological Demand Avoidance. Long words, but they do actually say something important.

Demand avoidance means that people with PDA get much more stressed than most people if they are asked to do something that someone else wants them to do. When this happens, we try to get out of doing these things because we are so stressed. We avoid the 'demand' that we feel. This makes it very hard for us to co-operate with everyday things. Sometimes it's almost impossible.

Now, everyone tries to get out of doing things some of the time. It may be annoying everyday things like tidying our bedrooms, doing homework or brushing our teeth. All children do this some of the time. Children with PDA do this much more often. And not just with the things that no one likes doing, but sometimes even things we might want to do, like getting ready to go to the cinema to watch a new film that we have been asking to see. Even when we want to do something, our PDA can get in the way of us managing to do it. "

"I often come up with excuses for
why I can't do what I'm asked."

"I might say:

- 'I'm sorry, but I'm too busy.'

- 'I've got tummy ache.' (Even if I haven't really.)

- 'I can't come...my legs don't work.'

- 'I will do it, just not now.'

- 'The cat doesn't like it when I tidy my bedroom.'

- 'You're really good at it, why don't you do it for me?!'

- 'I have just painted my nails so I don't want to chip them.'

- 'I read that if I don't wash my hair for long enough, it will clean itself.'

Sometimes when I say things like this they are a bit of an exaggeration!

I have been told that when I am trying to avoid doing something I seem unkind or selfish. I wish people understood that I don't mean to be. I don't feel unkind or selfish on the inside, I'm just trying to stop feeling anxious.

PDA affects the way people like me think, behave and learn at home and at school. It affects us when we are on our own and when we are with other people.

When I get anxious about doing something, I get totally focused on not doing that thing."

"When the anxiety gets too big I can have tantrums or outbursts. It's like a volcano of burning emotions spilling out like hot lava."

"If you saw me then you might notice me doing things that much younger children usually do, like shouting, stamping and lying on the floor. By the time I am like this, I can't stop myself and it can take me a long time to finish. Sometimes hours. It's horrid, but I will tell you more about this later.

Sometimes I can be so worried about being asked to do something that I get too stuck to do *anything*! Every child has some days when it's hard to do what they are being asked, but children with PDA find this *much* more difficult, *much* more often than most other people. That's what the word 'pathological' means. It is a way of describing something that happens *much* more than for most ordinary people.

Some days I am more sensitive than others. If I'm having a sensitive day, it means I'm quicker to get worried or scared. I need help to take the pressure off on those days and it doesn't always work out well. Although I feel really bad about it, sometimes when I get upset I break stuff and even hit people. Once, at home, I pushed my sister over and smashed the TV. We were all upset about that."

"People ask me how they can help me, so I will tell you what works for me. These ideas may also work for the person with PDA that you know.

It helps me if people let me know what I need to do without actually telling me what to do in a bossy way. My mum calls it being 'indirect', which means that it is best for me if I'm given choices or suggestions rather than instructions. I don't expect to never get instructions, but having them less often helps. I will tell you one example.

Mum and I used to fall out with each other over getting ready for school in the mornings. I don't know how Alice finds it so much easier than me to get ready. It is very hard for me to do all the things that need to happen before going to school, and for a long time it was so hard that on a good day I was late and on a bad day I missed school altogether. When I missed school I got bored at home, and annoyed that I had got stuck. Mum used to get stressed too because it meant she had to miss work.

We have worked out a few things that help me in the mornings. They don't all work every day but things are usually better now."

"Mum lets Splodge be the first to come into my bedroom in the mornings so he starts to wake me up a bit before anyone else does."

"Some things that help are:

- Mum sets out my clothes and packs my school bag the night before so I only have to choose my snack for break time.

- I can choose to have my breakfast in the kitchen, or in front of the TV or in my bedroom. Mum and Dad decided this was better than arguing about breakfast like we used to most days.

- Mum gives me a lift to school even though it is not far away. Alice prefers to walk with her friends but I can have longer to get ready if I go in the car.

- I have a bath and brush my teeth in the evening so that if I don't manage to wash or to brush my teeth in the morning it doesn't matter as much.

Another thing that helps me is if I know what is happening. I don't like routines to get boring but I do like to know what to expect. I like it when my day is explained so I'm prepared for any changes or choices in that day."

"Mrs Jones has a good system to help me do my school work. It's called 'projects on pause'. I call it 'projects on paws' so I can draw pictures of Splodge on the folder."

"If there is something I can't do that day, I can put it in the 'on pause' folder and either do it later or another day. I like choosing work from the folder. When I look back through the work in it it's hard to remember why I didn't want to do it when I first got it. The work is not too hard for me; I just couldn't cope with it that day I suppose.

I am really good at working on projects. I like having more than one project on the go at a time. That way, I can choose which one to do and who can help me. I can choose to work with Mrs Jones, Miss Mckenna or sometimes Emily.

Some days I'm fine and you wouldn't think I was any different from the other children. Those are good times because they are days when I am able to do well and to feel good. There are other days when I can't do well and I don't feel good.

I go to Lambton Grove School. There are 400 children at my school and 26 in my class. I'm in the last year at the school so next year I will go to Greengates School where there are more than 1000 children. Most of them will be bigger and older than me so I am a bit worried about my new school, but I have already started visiting so I am learning my way round. I already have my new uniform so I can get used to it. Sometimes I put it on for a while at home. I am trying to get to know some of the teachers too. It will help me if I can find a teacher who I get on well with before I actually start.

I am a clever person, but sometimes at school I find it hard to do the work. It isn't because the work is too hard; it's because some days are 'comfy slippers days' and others are 'sore feet days'. Luckily my teacher Mrs Jones knows me well and she understands. She is my best shield at school. Miss McKenna helps in our class too and she is nice. She is a kind of shield but not as strong as Mrs Jones."

"It's really important to me to be around people who make me feel safe and who understand me. I call these people my shields."

"They shield me from what they can when I can't cope. They let me just be myself. Even if I'm having a good day, it's *so* much better if one of my shields is around.

PDA affects me every day. It affects me in different ways in different places. For example, it's easier for me to get ready for the next activity at school. At home, it's easier for me to talk about my feelings.

Ideally, I need a shield in every situation. That means at home, at school, at a party, at the shops... wherever I am really. Mum says that's why it's important that people around me understand about PDA so that they know what sort of help I need. She also says that as I get older, I will need to get better at taking charge of looking after myself. At the moment I can't imagine being able to do that but hopefully that will change when I'm grown up.

My favourite people are the ones who can share a laugh with me, who can spot when I'm getting stressed, who understand me and who like me. These are the people who can be gentle and calm if I'm having a tough time, but who can also help me to move on past it. That doesn't mean that they only say things I want to hear; in fact I feel closer to them because they are the ones who are with me when things are going wrong as well as when things are great."

"If someone wants to say I've done well,
it's best if they tell someone else while I'm
listening without saying it right to me."

"I like other people to notice when I do well but this can also be really difficult for me. I want to be noticed, but I don't like having a fuss.

It makes me feel horrid if people say, 'Well done, Issy, aren't you brilliant, look what you have done!' because then everyone looks at me and starts to join in which I don't like at all. It also stresses me because then I worry that they will think I should be brilliant all the time and I know I can't be.

Otherwise, it's OK if they say it when I'm on my own as long as they don't go on about it. I would never want to go on the stage in a school assembly no matter how well I've done!"

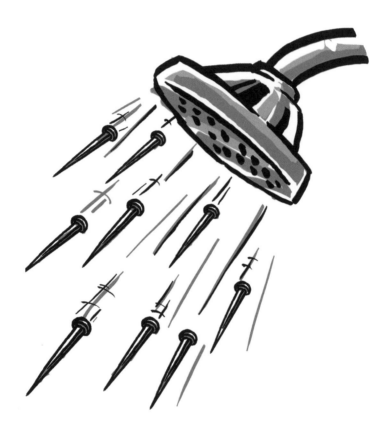

"I don't like showers because the water feels really sharp on my skin. That's why I have baths."

"Like some other people on the autism spectrum, I can be very sensitive to feelings from my senses such as strong smells and loud noises. In my case, I have a problem with the stiffness of new clothes and especially new shoes. When I get new clothes, they need to be washed lots of times before I can wear them. And they have to have no lumpy buttons or scratchy zips. School uniform used to be a big problem for me, but I have got used to it now.

Brushing my teeth has always been hard for me. I still use children's toothpaste because it's not so minty, and I use an electric toothbrush because it's not so scratchy in my mouth.

School can be a very noisy and smelly place for me. Sometimes that means I have real trouble paying attention in class. Shopping centres are bad for that too. And airports are even worse. I have to listen to my iPod in an airport and when we go on holiday we get there really early so it's not so busy."

"When Alfie gets really stressed he sometimes swears and hides in his wardrobe wrapped in his duvet."

"That makes it hard for him if he has a difficult moment and he is not at home. Once he ran away from his family in town and got lost. That was really scary.

I know that everyone gets stressed or anxious some of the time, but it happens to people with PDA much more often. It's not just if someone tells me to do something that I think might be hard, but if I'm asked to do something that I don't think needs doing, or something that I'm not ready for, or that I can't see the point in doing, I can get really stressed. I know that other children would feel some of this too, but they seem to have more ways to get over it than children like me or Alfie. I can also spend time feeling so worried about the next problem coming along that I can't enjoy what I'm doing right now.

When I get really anxious or stressed, these are some of the things I feel:

- My heart beats faster than usual.

- My body gets sweaty.

- My arms and legs start to tingle.

- I can't think straight.

- I don't seem to know what I want to say.

- I need to be in charge.

- I don't want people to talk to me or even look at me.

When I get very stressed Mum and Dad say I'm having a 'meltdown'. That's their word for describing what happens when I'm really not coping. It is quite a good word to describe it because it does feel like things around me are melting away and I have nothing secure left to hang on to. I usually feel scared when I'm having a meltdown, although other people say I look angry.

Sometimes when people ask me about a big meltdown I had, it's hard for me to remember what happened.

When I'm having a meltdown I often lie down on the floor. It makes me feel better to roll around and make noises like my cat. If I'm at home this is not too bad but it is a problem if I'm at school or out somewhere. Grown-ups can help me by backing off and giving me some space away from everyone. When I had a meltdown at school last week, Mrs Jones put a heavy blanket over my shoulders. I thought it was a weird thing to do at the time but it did actually help. I think I will try it again.

Sometimes my family or my teachers say they feel like I've over-reacted to them when I have had a problem doing what they ask me. They find it hard to accept that there are some days I just *can't*. These are not good days and the more they ask me, the more stuck I get.

As I get older I can tell when a bad day is already happening. I can't tell in advance, although my mum says it's more likely on a day that includes a haircut or a school trip or a party. I would really like to be able to cope better when I'm starting to get stressed so that it doesn't turn into a meltdown.

I hope that writing about PDA will help you understand anyone you know who is a bit like me.

Having PDA is only one part of my life. Although having PDA can cause some problems and is an important part of who I am, it is not the only thing people need to know about me. If someone wants to get to know *me*, they need to find out what I'm interested in and what I'm good at first. Then they can start finding out about how PDA affects my life.

PDA makes me different from people without PDA but it is also part of my way of being who I am. I don't think I would like to have my PDA taken away but I would like to find it easier to fit in with other people and to get better at managing my temper. I'm sure my family and teachers will be able to help me.

Dad says there are more than enough ordinary people in the world and that I'm unique to be in a special group of people with PDA. I like it when he says that because it makes me feel like a VIP. That means a Very Important Person. **"**

How other people can help

Anyone living or working with a child with PDA needs to remember that this condition is part of the autism spectrum. This means that although there will be a different emphasis in strategies used, it is not true that there is one list of strategies exclusively for children with autism and another separate list for children with PDA. Lots of children need a combination of the two, with individualised adaptations. The key to helping children and young people with PDA lies in looking closely at your style. *Changing the way you do things more than what you actually do can make all the difference.*

We describe this as developing an altered *approach* rather than developing a particular *system*. What we mean is that systems are structures to follow, such as schedules, which work very effectively with people who have more typical autism. An approach is about using a certain style or attitude in what you do, and it is by developing a flexible and less directive approach that you will engage best with someone with PDA.

There is often a range of adults involved in supporting a child with PDA at home and at school including professionals such as psychologists or social or health care workers. These people will all have different skills and perspectives, but there are some important things they can *all* do to help:

- Choose priorities carefully and collaboratively.

- Be less direct when you ask for something to be done.

- Be flexible in your approach.

- Build positive relationships with the child.

- Reduce the child's anxiety.

- Promote emotional wellbeing.

- Be creative and individualised.

- Be confident and clear.

- Give time and space.

- Manage meltdowns calmly and safely.

- Keep an eye on overload.

- Support making and keeping friends.

These will each be considered in more detail.

CHOOSE PRIORITIES CAREFULLY AND COLLABORATIVELY

Prioritise carefully which issues to address. There may be lots of things that you, as well as the child with PDA, wish were different. However, none of us can change lots of difficult things at the same time, so choose priorities that are urgent and realistic. Choose them together with the other people who support and live with the child. Decide how you are going to try to make changes and set your goals on small but significant steps forward. *Make your starting point an aim to understand the behaviour before you begin to challenge it.* That way, you will be more likely to find strategies that will make sense to the child, and therefore be more successful. If possible, include the child in new strategies. Ideally, include key people at home, at school and elsewhere so that you are able to work collaboratively. Also, in choosing priorities, be aware that you need to think ahead for the child as they move towards the next stage in their life, whatever that is, but particularly as they become a young person, and ultimately an adult.

BE LESS DIRECT WHEN YOU ASK FOR SOMETHING TO BE DONE

Be less direct when you make requests of a child with PDA; for example, rather than telling them to put their shoes on, ask them whether they want to put their shoes on sitting on the stairs *or* the chair, or ask them to surprise you with *which* pair of shoes they put on. If you would like them to do a task with you, try saying out loud that you wish you had someone nearby who could help you, or who could show you *how* to do the task.

These strategies are not suggesting an exact script to follow but are to illustrate a style.

Some children are very sensitive to praise, and these children may even need praising or rewarding indirectly. For example, within a child's hearing tell a friend or colleague or another family member what the child has achieved and how proud of them you are. Offer an unexpected treat to reward them by giving the treat to everyone for various achievements, including the child with PDA.

Another way of being indirect is to *depersonalise* a request, for example referring to an instruction manual, or external requirement or third-party document (even a worksheet) so that the request is not felt so directly as coming from you. For example, "The government and the United Nations (UN) say that children have to receive an education".

BE FLEXIBLE IN YOUR APPROACH

Be flexible in how you present a task or activity or appointment. Be prepared to adjust your expectations depending on the situation.

It may help to imagine a set of two dials.

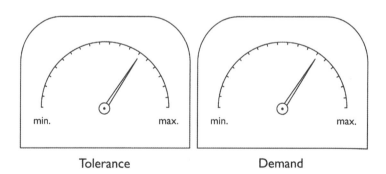

Tolerance   Demand

One dial represents the child's tolerance at any given time, and the other represents the demand (including the perceived demand) that you are presenting to the child. Try to synchronise the dials so that although you can increase your demand if the child's tolerance rises, you are also able to lower your demand if their tolerance drops.

Allow opportunities for alternative ways of doing things that preserve the priority goal but offer flexibility regarding the details. Be prepared to postpone some things if the emerging battle is not one worth fighting at that time. If, on the other hand, it is something worth seeing through, allow plenty of time so as to reduce pressure on yourself and the child. Think about what will make sense to the child at that time and use your understanding of them to present the task in a way that will be acceptable to them. Sometimes issues need to be carried through and there is a time and a place for this, especially regarding safety. Other times, retaining enough flexibility within an event or a task to come to a mutually satisfactory conclusion is the best way to achieve a good outcome for everyone.

BUILD POSITIVE RELATIONSHIPS WITH THE CHILD

Be an active member of the team that supports the child. This team will include parents, possibly siblings or other family members, and all involved professionals. Talk often and openly to one another. Learn about PDA as well as about each individual child. Recognise the strain that adults are under in living and working with children with PDA. Understand that these children can often be very different at home from at school. Keep up to date about what are the most important things *to* the child and *for* the child. Be a positive member of the team and prioritise building good relationships with the child. Not only will positive relationships benefit the child's wellbeing, they will enhance your interactions and will maximise the chances of co-operation because the child will feel more secure.

REDUCE THE CHILD'S ANXIETY

A child with PDA wants to do well if they can even though it often doesn't feel like that. If they are not managing very well, it probably means they are getting stressed, in which case they won't be feeling good about how things are going or about how they are behaving. If you can help to reduce anxiety you will definitely be increasing the chance of them coping and co-operating. You will also be improving the tone of interactions with everyone involved. As they mature, children with PDA will need to learn ways to manage their own anxiety. This may include physical exercise, something distracting to take out with them such as an electronic toy/gadget, a hobby or having a way to leave stressful situations *before* the crucial point of meltdown.

PROMOTE EMOTIONAL WELLBEING

Promote emotional wellbeing by helping the child to understand their emotions and to develop their own ways of dealing with these emotions. Work on strategies that will help them to cope when their emotions are intense, but before their emotions become overwhelming. Young adults with PDA often describe having as much difficulty dealing with happy or excited feelings as they do dealing with angry or anxious feelings. A problem can be in a fundamental difficulty understanding and moderating emotions, whether positive or negative.

It might be helpful to start with work that recognises and describes emotions away from the times when they are actually experiencing those emotions. This work could be done in relation to themselves as well as other people. It may help to use examples of other people or TV shows/films to depersonalise the issues. It is often helpful to develop a sliding scale of intensity of different feelings alongside outcomes or strategies for managing these experiences. It might be useful to grade feelings, for example from 0 to 5 with 3 representing neutral feelings, 0 negative and 5 positive. This idea can also be helpful to grade preferences as well as behaviours or consequences. Using visual approaches such as drawing, barometers and visual images or analogies can help here, as can using puppets or role play.

Looking ahead, it is really important as children mature that they develop a self-awareness that values and celebrates their uniqueness and skills, while also being aware of aspects of life that they find challenging. If the sort of strategies described here are personalised, used regularly and over time, they can lead to young people developing an understanding of who they are, a positive sense of themselves as an individual and an awareness of when and what help they require. At some point, this will inevitably include an awareness of their own condition and how it affects them.

BE CREATIVE AND INDIVIDUALISED

Be *creative* and *individualised* in finding ways to motivate and connect with a child with PDA. We all work best, and co-operate more willingly, when we are doing something we are interested in with people we enjoy being around. Use a fun approach, a sense of humour, a range of options, novelty, role play and drama to be appealing. For adults a child with PDA gives us lots of opportunities to explore different ways of presenting tasks and teaching. Often learning alongside the child, or even getting them to teach you something, can also be helpful.

BE CONFIDENT AND CLEAR

Take care to let the child know what is happening in their day or environment so that they don't get unwelcome surprises which could raise their anxiety. For example, let them know if there are visitors to the house or to school; let them know if there will be workmen carrying out repairs especially if they may be noisy; let them know if there are unusual arrangements that day such as a school trip or an appointment. Be *clear but not bossy* and stay *flexible* about the things that are open for negotiation. Be *confident* in how you present the things that are not open for negotiation. Children with PDA need a degree of flexibility, but they also need the security of having some boundaries which are the bottom line. If the adults around them are not clear and confident about these agreed minimum rules or boundaries, the child will only be more anxious.

GIVE TIME AND SPACE

Give the child *time* and *space*. They may need time and space to process the information you have given them for two reasons: first, so that they understand the content of what you have said, and second to get used to the idea of co-operating with it.

If you rush them when they have either not quite understood, or not quite accepted a request, their anxiety will be raised and their co-operation will be lowered. They may also need some time and space if they need to calm themselves once they have become upset. Find a way of creating this time and space that works for the child in various situations. Remember too that giving the child time and space also gives you time and space as well so that you can gather your thoughts and make any necessary adaptations.

MANAGE MELTDOWNS CALMLY AND SAFELY

Managing meltdowns can be challenging and complicated. It is of course always preferable to prevent them, but the first priority when that has not been possible is to keep everyone safe. It is really helpful if you can stay calm yourself, even if you are feeling frustrated or worried. That doesn't mean that you have to put up with unreasonable or unpleasant behaviour, it just means that reacting emotionally yourself won't help anyone. Children with PDA tend to meet confrontation with confrontation. Find ways of releasing and soothing your own emotions. Equally, find ways of showing the child what you will accept and what you cannot accept. Wherever possible, *challenge the child in a calm and considered manner.*

KEEP AN EYE ON OVERLOAD

There may be additional stress factors that aren't immediately obvious. These may include information overload, taking things literally, feeling unwell, being confused by a social situation and experiencing a lower tolerance to demands or sensory overload.

These things will be hard for someone with PDA to recognise or communicate as well as to process. When any of us is reaching overload for whatever reason, we find it harder to communicate, to cope and to control our emotions. When a child with PDA feels like this, you will have to do some of the problem solving for them.

SUPPORT MAKING AND KEEPING FRIENDS

Children with PDA usually want to have friends but often struggle to understand the give and take that a friendship requires. Teach a child with PDA that they are valued and good company. Show them that you see the best in them and that other people want to be around them. Teach them how to be a good friend, who are good choices of friends, and how to repair a disagreement with a friend so that they can learn to sustain positive relationships over time. Sometimes children with PDA get along much better with children younger than them – this may be because they feel less threatened by younger children so they are less tense. Most children with PDA are chatty and can come across as socially confident. This is not always what is really happening. Some children with PDA may not spot when other children are being unkind if those other children are giving them attention, so help them see the signs of positive as well as negative relationships.

Recommended reading, organisations and websites

PUBLICATIONS

Al-Ghani, K.I. and Al-Ghani, H. (2008) *The Red Beast: Controlling Anger in Children with Asperger's Syndrome.* London: Jessica Kingsley Publishers.

Autism Education Trust (AET) (2012) *AET National Autism Standards for Schools and Educational Settings.* London: Autism Education Trust. Available at www.aettraininghubs. org.uk/wp-content/uploads/2012/06/AET-National-Autism-Standards_distributed.pdf, accessed on 19 November 2014.

Buron, K.D. and Curtis, M. (2003) *The Incredible 5-Point Scale: Assisting Students with Autism Spectrum Disorders in Understanding Social Interactions and Controlling Their Emotional Responses.* Shawnee Mission, KS: Autism Asperger Publishing.

Christie, P., Duncan, M., Fidler, R. and Healy, Z. (2012) *Understanding Pathological Demand Avoidance Syndrome in Children: A Guide for Parents, Teachers and Other Professionals.* London: Jessica Kingsley Publishers.

Davis, J. (1993) *Children with Pathological Demand Avoidance Syndrome: A Booklet for Brothers and Sisters.* Nottingham: Elizabeth Newson Centre.

Greene, R.W. (2005) *The Explosive Child.* New York, NY: HarperCollins.

Huebner, D. (2006) *What to Do When You Worry Too Much – A Kid's Guide to Overcoming Anxiety.* Washington: Magination Press.

Ironside, V. (1996) *The Huge Bag of Worries.* London: Hodder.

Lipsky, D. and Richards, W. (2009) *Managing Meltdowns.* London: Jessica Kingsley Publishers.

Plummer, D. (2007) *Helping Children to Build Self-Esteem.* London: Jessica Kingsley Publishers.

Welton, J. (2004) *Can I Tell You About Asperger Syndrome? A Guide for Friends and Family.* London: Jessica Kingsley Publishers.

Welton, J. (2014) *Can I Tell You About Autism? A Guide for Friends, Family and Professionals.* London: Jessica Kingsley Publishers.

Whitehouse, E. and Pudney, W. (1996) *A Volcano in My Tummy – Helping Children to Handle Anger.* Gabriola Island, BC: New Society Publishers.

ORGANISATIONS

UK

Autism Education Trust (AET)

c/o National Autistic Society
393 City Road
London
EC1V 1NG
Phone: 020 7903 3650
Email: info@autismeducationtrust.org.uk
Website: www.autismeducationtrust.org.uk

The Autism Education Trust (AET) was launched in November 2007 with funding from the Department for Children, Schools and Families (DCSF). It is dedicated to co-ordinating and improving education support for all children on the autism spectrum in England.

The National Autistic Society

393 City Road
London
EC1V 1NG
Phone: 020 7833 2299
Email: nas@nas.org.uk
Website: www.autism.org.uk

The leading UK charity for people on the autism spectrum and their families. They provide information, support, education and a range of services.

NORSACA
Park Hall Autism Resource Centre
Park Road
Bestwood Village
Nottingham
NG6 8TQ
Phone: 0115 976 1805
Website: www.norsaca.org.uk

NORSACA is a charity based in the East Midlands which provides information, support, education and a range of services to people on the autism spectrum and their families. It includes the Elizabeth Newson Centre and Sutherland House School.

PDA Society
Email: info@pdasociety.org.uk
Website: www.pdasociety.org.uk

The PDA Society was initially set up as the PDA Contact Group in 1997 by parents. It became the PDA Society in 2014. It provides information, resources and support to families and professionals. Although a UK-based organisation it is open to people from all countries.

There are many international autism organisations who can be contracted for more general information about the autism spectrum.

USA

Autism Society
4340 East-West Hwy, Suite 350
Bethesda
Maryland 20814
Phone: (301) 657 0881 or 1 800 3AUTISM (1 800 328 8476)
Email: see form on website
Website: www.autism-society.org

The Autism Society is the leading grassroots autism organization in the USA and hopes to improve the lives of all affected by autism.

CANADA

Autism Society Canada
Box 22017
1670 Heron Road
Ottawa
Ontario
K1V 0W2
Phone: (613) 789 8943
Toll-free: 1 866 476 8440
Email: info@autismsocietycanada.ca
Website: www.autismsocietycanada.ca

Autism Society Canada works to reduce the impact of ASDs on individuals and their families.

AUSTRALIA

Autism Spectrum Australia (Aspect)
Aspect, PO Box 361
Forestville
NSW 2087
Phone: 1 800 277 328
Website: www.autismspectrum.org.au

Autism Spectrum Australia (Aspect) is Australia's leading service provider for autism and other disabilities.

NEW ZEALAND

Autism New Zealand Inc. National Office
Level 1, Master Builders Building
271–277 Willis Street
Wellington 6011
Postal address: PO Box 6455
Marion Square
Wellington 6141
Phone: 0800 AUTISM (288 476) *or* +64 4 803 3501
Email: info@autismnz.org.nz
Website: www.autismnz.org.nz

Autism New Zealand Inc. provides support, training, advocacy, resources and information on Autism Spectrum disorders including Aspergers Syndrome.

EUROPE

Autism Europe
Rue Montoyer 39 bte 11
1000 Brussels
Belgium
Phone: +32 (0) 2 675 7505
Email: secretariat@autismeurope.org
Website: www.autismeurope.org

Autism-Europe aisbl is an international association whose main objective is to advance the rights of people with autism and their families and to help them improve their quality of life.

REPUBLIC OF IRELAND

Irish Autism Action
41 Newlands
Mullingar
Co. Westmeath
Phone: +353 (0) 44 9331609
Email: kevin1aa@ircom.net
Website: www.autismireland.ie

Formed in 2001, Irish Autism Action brings positive change into the lives of those affected by autism. They are an umbrella organisation with over 40 member groups and also individual members.